Andrea Schwartz

Lessons Learned

FROM YEARS OF HOMESCHOOLING

*A Christian Mother Shares Her Insights from
a Quarter Century of Teaching Her Children*

THE CHALCEDON FOUNDATION · VALLECITO, CALIFORNIA

Chalcedon / Ross House Books
PO Box 158
Vallecito, CA 95251
www.chalcedon.edu

Library of Congress Catalog Card Number: 2006901856
ISBN: 9781891375248

Printed in the United States of America

To my parents Anthony and Marie
for faithfully seeing to it
that I received an excellent academic education

To my spiritual parents Rush and Dorothy
for instructing and mentoring me
on the importance of Christian education

To my husband Ford
and my children Anthony, Rachel, and Dorothy
who have helped me become the teacher I am today

TABLE OF CONTENTS

Acknowledgments

As a result of my association with the Chalcedon Foundation, I have been blessed to become acquainted with a number of people whose life work inspires me. Years ago, Sam Blumenfeld, one such individual, during a yearly visit to California, encouraged me to write a book about my homeschooling adventures. At the time, I had been homeschooling for only eleven years, had yet to have any graduates, and felt the idea, at best, to be a humorous one.

Fast-forward the clock to the summer of 2005 when Chris Ortiz, editor of *Faith for All of Life*, the Chalcedon magazine, exhorted me to share my homeschooling insights and experiences of almost a quarter century with others. He asked me (if you know Chris, it was more like a commission) to write a series of essays for the Chalcedon Foundation website (www.chalcedon.edu). Over half of the collection in this book is a result of that request. The rest consist of essays that were written and published previously.

Then there is Bob Voss, a friend, who delivered some faithful wounds back in 1983 to my husband and me as we were demonstrating a decided lack of any orthodox understanding of Scripture or what it truly meant to be a Christian. As a result of his "pointed remarks" and the care and concern to follow them up with a reading list which included the writings of R.J. Rushdoony (known as the father of the Christian school and homeschooling movement), we began what was a definitive turning point and ultimate inspiration to make our Christian faith something that would end up permeating every area of our lives and thoughts.

And, where would I be today had I not had the benefit of sitting under the teaching and hands-on instruction of Dr. Rushdoony, "Rush," and his wife Dorothy, as we sat for hours and hours talking, asking questions, laughing, and growing in the Christian faith. Among the very good reasons for desiring heaven is to see both of these dear saints again.

There are countless others who have played important roles in the formulation of this series of essays—friends, co-workers, authors I've read, preachers I've listened to, movies I've seen, even those who'd be surprised to find themselves on my list of those I wished to thank. And, while my name appears as the author of this collection, in a very real sense my husband and children are entitled to ghost-writing credit as they participated as integral parts of the entire homeschool experience that has allowed me to have anything to offer in the way of guidance or counsel.

And finally, it would be a grievous oversight to omit my gratitude to that Person who knows my sins and weaknesses better than anyone else, and yet allows me to participate in that great work of building the Kingdom of God.

INTRODUCTION

Over the years, I have received many a quizzical look when people learn that I homeschool. However, once they discover that I have successfully homeschooled two of my three children through high school, the look usually becomes one of awe. Then I invariably hear, "Gee, I could never do that!" Funny thing is, when I first heard about homeschooling, my first thought was, "Gee, people do that? That's something I'd love to do!"

No one I knew homeschooled. In fact, my husband's first reaction was to let me know in no uncertain terms that what I wanted to do was fine for our son's preschool years, but when he was at kindergarten or first grade age, we would have to re-evaluate the whole idea. By the time that day rolled around, my husband was solidly on board—even facetiously taking credit for the original idea. My own father (who had obediently sent me to parochial school in response to instructions given in his pre-marital counseling with my mother) was not at peace with this notion of mine. Yet now, at the age of ninety-four, is as proud as he can be with the success of his homeschooled grandchildren.

In looking back at almost twenty-five years of taking responsibility for the education of my children, there are a number of things which I credit with sustaining me through it. First, and foremost is the grace of the Holy Spirit in giving me the inspiration and perseverance to keep my *hands to the plow* as I taught myself and learned from others how to be a resourceful, effective teacher. What a blessing it was and is to know that I'm not in this alone— that He who began a good work in me will see it through until the day of Christ Jesus!

Secondly, it was the providence of God to encounter the writings of R.J. Rushdoony and publications of the Chalcedon Foundation. Although I don't have any credentials from any college or university, through Chalcedon I have been a steadfast student of the Word and Christian education for the past twenty-one years. It is precisely this underpinning that has made it possible for me to further the cause of Jesus Christ by furthering the goals of education from a distinctively Christian point of view. Books like *The Philosophy of the Christian Curriculum, The Messianic Character of American Education, Institutes of Biblical Law*, and *Revolt Against Maturity* have all helped to stabilize me in the all-too-real spiritual battles that pursuing a Christian education for my children has led me.

Because of my longevity in this very noble activity, I've come to be a contact point for people embarking on this route for the first time, or struggling with their decision or capabilities. I routinely begin by asking, "Would you say that you qualify as a mediocre teacher?" Customarily, the answer is a hesitant, "No, I think I'm better than mediocre." I then say, "Well, for the sake of argument, let's call you a mediocre teacher. Who do you think has a better chance of getting a better education—one student with a mediocre teacher or thirty-plus students with a superior teacher?" The answer, usually accompanied by a snicker, reveals that my listener gets my point all too well. I further make the case that even the best teachers don't have time to pour themselves into each and every student. As my son, now married and established in business, says when asked if he thought his being homeschooled had any disadvantages replies, "No, actually, I think it has given me an unfair advantage!" One, I might add, he appreciates having.

It is truly a testimony to the indoctrination of our modern culture that parents deem themselves unqualified to teach. After all, they did manage to be the starting point for such monumental teaching tasks for their children as walking, talking, toilet-training, and dressing themselves. But, when it comes to imparting the disciplines of academics (which most have successfully gone through themselves to one degree or another), they are *certain* that they must defer to the experts. Imagine that! A person who can read, write, and compute is categorically unable to instruct one's own child in the same. That sort of begs the question: if your own education didn't take root, why are you willing to sacrifice your children's in the same way?

Of course, it is well documented that homeschooled students fare as well or better than their counterparts in private or public schools, and, with their teachers having far less credentials and letters after their names than the professional counterparts. So, there must be something very workable in a homeschool setting. But, I would venture to say there is much, much more to the story.

What makes *Christian* homeschooling work so well is that it has its foundation in the understanding that our children are given to us by God to steward and direct their lives to His honor and glory. And that's a good thing because, without such a premise and foundation, the entire enterprise would be doomed to failure.

It is my sincere hope that as you take a peek into the window of my homeschool experience, you will realize that it doesn't take a superior person to homeschool children: it takes the Supreme Being to allow you to succeed by means of His Son and His strength.

I

PARENT-DIRECTED
CHRISTIAN EDUCATION

Training children is an all-encompassing, time-consuming enterprise given to parents by God (Deut. 6:1–7). Both quality time and quantity time are required. This Biblical mandate extends to *every area of life* so that all thoughts are brought into captivity to the obedience of Jesus Christ and His Word and rule (2 Cor. 10:5). God charges parents with the responsibility and authority to nurture their children in the fear and admonition of the Lord.

For education to be truly Biblical, godly teachers must instruct children with God-honoring and life-equipping principles and materials so they become productive members of the Kingdom of God. Training in *all* disciplines and subjects must reflect basic principles of Scripture: that we have no other gods before God (e.g., career advancement, addictions, or lusts); that we not bow down to any ideology or system in place of God (e.g., feminism, libertarianism, or environmentalism); that we not take God's name in vain by giving lip service to the faith while our speech and dress oppose God's standards; that honoring our parents is more important than being accepted by our peers, etc. In addition, children must be taught the fear of the Lord and that *nothing* should be considered acceptable if it denies the truth of Scripture. In essence, they must know with certainty that the *Faith* is for *all* of life.

Psalm 127 teaches that children are God's heritage. God gives specific children to specific parents and *not* to the state. Parents who surrender this stewardship responsibility and privilege to secularism disobey the clear commands of Scripture. No matter how ill equipped they may think they are for the task, their parental responsibility (and culpability) remains. All parents will stand before the Lord one day and give an account for how they prepared their children for service in the Kingdom of God. Good grades, high test scores, and college scholarships will not impress God. Whereas those are all beneficial, they will take their proper place behind the child's ability to explain *how* and *why* Jesus is the way, the truth, and the life in all disciplines and areas of study.

Where this education takes place is secondary to *that* it takes place. Parents may decide to "out source" education, but this does not relieve them of their responsibility to oversee their child's education. They may want a better level of instruction for their children than they can give and hire tutors for specific subjects (calculus or chemistry, for example), or they may enroll their children in a Christian school. However they decide, they must understand that the piano teacher, athletic instructor, tutor, or schoolteacher is *not* ultimately responsible for the content and application of what is being studied. They, as parents, are.

The options are many: day schools, correspondence courses, homeschools, or co-operative school settings. Support from both the church and those "veterans" who already have made the journey is vital.

The Scriptures tell us to train up a child in the way he should go, and when he is old he will not depart from it (Prov. 22:6). This is not an unconditional promise, but rather wisdom that reaffirms *what we sow in our children is what we will reap to ourselves and our culture.*

2

TAKING THE PLUNGE

Homeschooling has gained more acceptance since 1982, the year I took the plunge and began my career as a homeschooling mom. I had seen a man being interviewed on television, who had written a book about parents teaching their own children rather than sending them to day schools. My son was four at the time, and people just figured I was suffering from a separation anxiety that I'd soon get over. Even family members considered it a phase I was going through and kept checking up on me to see if I had progressed.

As my son got older, he was instructed not to make a big deal about our method of schooling, since it often produced long discussions and explanations for which we didn't always have the time for or inclination to address. Many folks (sometimes even strangers), when they found out we homeschooled, would cross-examine him. He became adept at politely answering the small-talk questions of cashiers or waitresses, such as "Are there many boys and girls in your class?" with a coy reply of "Not too many." Or, "Do you like your teacher better this year than last year?" with "Oh yes, she's much nicer."

My particular reasons for homeschooling evolved and matured over the years as I discovered Scriptural support for my decision. The same is true for homeschooling itself since more and more people either know families who educate this way or have seen the notable spelling or geography bee winners in the media who have been home taught. Now, instead of being viewed as some kooky, off-beat lifestyle, those who approach me are sure it's a wonderful way to educate, but point out that they don't have the "stuff" it takes to do it. Many are conscience torn as they feel God calling them to pursue this option, but feel grossly under-qualified or under-motivated for the endeavor.

The solution is to "take the plunge." Slowly making your way into a cold ocean or swimming pool prolongs the agony and makes you uncomfortable for an extended period of time; but totally submerging yourself quickly results in acclimation to the water's temperature. Similarly, many parents discover that once they "dive right in," the arctic waters they had imagined were really tropical pools.

But what about qualifications and curriculum and socialization? Before I tackle those, let's go back to the cold-water analogy. Do you have to be an Olympic class swimmer to get wet? Is perfect knowledge of the basic swimming strokes a prerequisite to going underwater? First things need to come first. Decide you are going to proceed, and learn as you go. Isn't that what parents do with their first child anyway? Who taught you how to talk to your child? Who instructed you how to figure out what different cries meant? What course did you take to make a boo-boo feel better? Truth be told, you *just did it!* Thankfully, there is a better road map than that after more than a quarter of a century of parents just like you educating their children themselves. An Internet search will provide much more information than you could possibly peruse in a month of doing nothing else. Moreover, there are many support groups, umbrella schools, and friendly people in every state and most countries willing to offer counsel and encouragement.

Once a family follows through with the decision to homeschool and gets started, questions and problems will arise. But that would be true with a day school setting as well. The remedy isn't to abandon the decision, but to commit to making yourself the best parent-educator you can be. I've yet to see a decision that is made prayerfully and based on Scripture where the Lord isn't right there, just as He promised, as a light for the path.

3

SETTING THE STANDARD

Sam Blumenfeld is a very smart man. I tend to listen to what he says. Recently, I had occasion to share a meal with Sam and during the course of our discussion, the subject of homeschooling came up again and again. As I was relating some of my experiences, he said, "When are you going to write your book? You really should."

Well, a book is a bit of an undertaking considering the fact that I am not without many things that take up my time, not the least of which is home educating my children. However, there are some insights and experiences that I feel eager to share based on my years of homeschooling. The fact that I have been at this for a number of years doesn't mean that my ways of doing things are any better than anyone else's. Nor does it mean that what worked for me will work the same way for others. What will be true, regardless of who homeschools and what situations or circumstances that they may find themselves, is that Jesus Christ is sovereign and Lord of all. Thus, anyone who undertakes the calling to home education done to the honor and glory of God should rest assured that He will never leave you nor forsake you nor ever let you go.

The most common tendency for homeschooling moms is to feel that they are competing with public educators in terms of the grades or accomplishments of their students. This has its positive points in that the home teacher wants to have a standard to assess the progress of her children. The problem, of course, is that the state schools are the wrong standard by which to judge. Sure, we want our children to be able to read and write and compute and think. Certainly, we want them to be trained well enough to find work when they are older that both serves the Kingdom of God and supports a family. However, if we make academic achievement the touchstone from which to judge how well we are doing, we have bought into the lie that education is what makes people good. Our faith and the Scriptures tell us differently. Without a living faith in Jesus Christ manifested by a life sanctified to Him by means of observing His law, no one can be saved. This is true despite how well the individual scores on achievement or SAT tests or how many trophies may be won in individual or team sports. The measure of goodness must be defined in terms of the Word of God. Am I saying that academic achievement and athletic accomplishments are not important? Quite the contrary. Often it is through one or both that an individual finds his or her calling under God. But to make these scores the measure, reflects a humanistic presupposition that states that character and faith are less important than secular rankings.

A homeschool should be focused at all times on the character of the individuals that comprise it. For this reason, it has always been an underlying premise in our home that *learning is a privilege not a right*. Whenever one of the children has displayed an attitude or manifestation inconsistent with godly standards, the academic subject ceases and the attitude is dealt with. Some might shudder and say, "Then my kids would be so far behind in their work!" Well, maybe they would, but are we really trying to produce better educated heathens? Isn't the most important subject in the curriculum the study and application of the Word of God? You'll be amazed at how much learning doesn't take place when the attitude is faulty and how maximized the time is when the attitude is right. We have even resorted to suspending the children from homeschool if the situation didn't correct itself readily. With increased focus on household jobs and projects (not all of which are pleasant), the children eventually requested (sometimes begged) to be allowed back.

Very early on in the homeschool, and family life in general, doctrine should be taught and established as the standard by which things are judged. I have, with much success, used the Westminster Shorter Catechism (with Scripture proofs) to firmly establish the faith with my children so that when the inevitable infractions come about, we can refer to the appropriate Scripture discussing how and why what took place was sin. (As an aside, you can incorporate this Bible and doctrine study with other academic subjects if you use the question and answer format for handwriting practice, dictation practice, and memorization. You can take care of a number of these language areas all at the same time and not feel tied to workbooks and other texts when the catechism can serve in a variety of ways. And the language of the catechism is so beautiful, clear, and to the point that it will improve your children's writing and speaking vocabulary.)

Never confuse a homeschool with utopia or paradise. Most veterans of a year or more would *never* make that mistake! Simply put, homeschool is very much like every other aspect of life. There are good days and bad days. There are joyous successes, dismal failures, but most often slow, steady progress. Keeping in mind on what standard we will judged, and Who will do the judging, we would be better served to stop competing with the world and renew our focus on serving our Master.

4

WALKING THE TALK

When all is said and done, children learn much more by observing what a parent does than by hearing what a parent says. This parallels Jesus's instruction to "Let your light so shine before men that they may *see* your good works," rather than a perspective that states, "Talk about light, and show why proper lighting is important." All parents must appreciate that they are engaged in an ongoing performance before their children. This performance needs to have content that is communicated with conviction and done consistently. Wait! Don't panic! No one I know (including myself) gets rave marks in this area all the time. That however doesn't alter the reality that actions scream louder than words and that the presence or absence of an unswerving Biblical witness in all areas of our lives is especially on display in the homeschool setting.

I don't intend to go into detail here about how the moral and ethical actions of parents need to be in harmony with their instruction to their children. The Scriptures repeatedly address making one's confession of faith match one's profession of faith. However, this concept is also relevant to academic issues. Parents need to guard against giving lip service to the importance of a subject or course of study that they themselves refuse to do. Your students will see right through the charade of "you need to be a good reader" when they never see you read anything more than the sports or gardening sections of the newspaper or your daily e-mail. Telling a child how necessary it is to do well in math, but responding to requests for assistance in Algebra with the retort, "I can't do that very well. It's just not my thing. Why don't you ask someone else?" gives the message that mathematics must not be so important. After all, you seem to be doing okay in life without it! Like it or not, the contradictions in our lives often overshadow those areas where our witness is reliable.

This begs the questions: what exactly makes up a good course of study? Should it be dictated by the state or some private educational institution? What is the end result you are going for? I've heard the expression time and again that if you don't know where you are going, any road will take you there. Homeschooling parents need to search the Scriptures and seek the guidance of faithful believers to ascertain what a godly education consists of. My experience tells me that this kind of effort will raise one's definition of education and enable you to make deliberate rather than casual choices when it comes to curriculum decisions.

So, how *do* you know if you are on the right road? The answers vary depending on where you are on the journey. However, an honest assessment of your commitment to raising your children in the fear and admonition of the Lord (in all areas of life, including academic subject matter), along with an accurate evaluation of how well prepared you are to teach your children, is essential.

SOME GENERAL GUIDELINES

Parents of children in infant/toddler stage:
Now is the time to assess your own academic skills. If you had a good education, then it is a matter of brushing up on skills stored in the dusty attic of your mind. If you didn't (and many graduates of public schools didn't), now is the time to lay a sturdy foundation in areas you failed to learn years before. With the number of Christian publishers who specifically gear their textbooks for home-

schoolers (text, teacher prompts, and answer key), there is really no significant barrier to getting yourself ready for teaching grammar school subjects. And, *no*, a degree in education is not mandatory in order to teach the basics of your own language and the principles of arithmetic to your child. If you can do it yourself, you can teach it. What's more, since your children are still quite young, you can further prepare yourself by reading books on teaching philosophy and practice.[1] You might even find opportunities to "apprentice" your skills as you help other homeschooling families.

Parents of school age children:

The same advice given above applies, but you may have to also make use of a homeschooling co-op situation because you don't have as much lead time. This is a particularly useful tool to handle subject matter in areas you feel less-than-adequate to teach. Put any group of committed parents together, and you'll find a mom or dad who has ample background in many areas (engineers, nurses, former teachers) and can help construct a good syllabus and course of study for you to work with your child on days that the co-op doesn't meet. Another option is part-time enrollment in a day school that provides enrichment classes for homeschoolers. My only MUST in this area is to have subjects you cannot teach adequately yourself taught by people who LOVE that subject. Nothing replaces enthusiasm and devotion in imparting something you love to another, especially a young person. Don't worry; these folks are out there. You'd be amazed at how many would love the opportunity to teach. Who knows? Those subjects you currently dread might actually seem more appealing once you understand the things you missed in your own school days!

Additionally, don't fall in love with *all* the decisions you make. Feel free to revise and revamp as needed. What works for one child, won't necessarily work for another. What is the appropriate learning style one year might well change as the child matures. Be flexible with the details, but be steadfast in the goal.

---

1. See *The Philosophy of the Christian Curriculum* by R.J. Rushdoony and *How to Tutor* by Sam Blumenfeld.

Make the commitment that you will never assign pointless tasks or busywork to your child. I recall when my son was just beginning to write essays that he would balk about putting all the time and effort into writing something only to have it put in a folder that no one else ever looked at. He had a great point: I wouldn't have subjected myself to that. So, I began to send his grandfather his essays, which gave my son an incentive to write. (Often Grandpa sent royalties of one to five dollars to encourage my essayist!) As he got older, this didn't satisfy. So I told my son that if he wrote, I would publish what he wrote. That gave birth to the *Kids for Life Newsletter* that had a run of about five years and ended up being circulated in our own community and had subscribers around the country. Needless to say, besides helping his writing improve, we were establishing a solid Biblical view of the evil of abortion as he and other young people constantly found fresh, innovative ways to express themselves on this topic.

Finally, let your children know if you struggle with a subject. Rather than reduce your authority or status with them, it will communicate that you are willing to work through something difficult so they can learn and gain a mastery of it. With all the resources of people, publishers, and other parents available, you should have no trouble getting questions answered and some real help when you need it. What's more, you'll be showing your children/students the importance of what is being studied because *you* are studying it *with them*. Or, if you are unable to master it enough to teach, you'll be demonstrating that you are willing to seek out tutors who can assist them. You'll be communicating that you deem their studies important enough to shell out the resources of time and/or money. Interestingly enough, if you're like me, you'll discover that one of the greatest by-products of homeschooling is that you become a more informed, well-educated individual yourself!

5

ARMING YOUR CHILDREN

Back in 1984, my husband and I enrolled our son in karate classes after a week at Vacation Bible School at a church we were attending; he had come home from VBS each day talking about the kid who kept taking his stuff and pushing him around. "I did that turn-the-other-cheek thing, Mom, that's in the Bible, but he just does it more." My husband thought it best that we become proactive, teaching our son how to defend himself against bullies, taking to heart something his dad (a World War I decorated veteran) had instilled in him, "Don't start a fight, but never walk away from one." As important a lesson as that was for me as a parent to learn in the physical realm, it has tremendous practical implications in all areas of life and thought. For if we fail to "arm" our children with the weapons God has ordained for them (and us) to use in defense against the onslaughts of the enemy, we will indeed be walking away from or defeated by the spiritual battles we are involved in daily.

From a very early age, my children were exposed to Bible story books. When they were able to read, I began to study individual books of the Bible (KJV) with them as part of our home-school curriculum. As we went along, we discussed the issues, implications, and imperatives contained in what R.J. Rushdoony calls "God's law-word." We wouldn't take on too big a chunk at any one time—just enough so that we had something to discuss and digest. My kids grew to understand that every word of Scripture serves as a command or mandate from our King. Thus, ignorance was never going to be an acceptable excuse, since God had given us His rule for our lives and contained it all in a book the size of which we could carry. This is how one begins to *think Biblically* and how *dominion* actually takes place.

There is a possible downside to all of this that I feel compelled to warn you about. That is, once your children begin to think Biblically, you have to learn to deal with questions and challenges to decisions you make and opinions you hold based on what the Word of God has to say. I've had some pretty lively discussions as my children progressed in years, as certain passages of Scripture were used to justify or explain a certain behavior or decision. However, if they were going to cite passages from the Bible, I made it a requirement that they had to properly exegete (explain the verse in context) as part of their plea. There were times I had to back down and reevaluate a particular issue based on their effective argumentation.

This *arming process* will serve your homeschooled children in good stead when they venture beyond your tutelage into the world of junior college and the university—whether secular or Christian. For every subject and profession, if it is to be truly learned and lived out to the glory of God, must view all tenets, practices, and policies from a thoroughly Biblical point of view. My son, many years after that bully at VBS, encountered a challenge in his job by being ordered to solicit business from an organization that, at its core, was wicked. He informed his employer that he would not sell to this account. When threatened with being fired, he stuck to his guns. Subsequently, when members of his sales team threatened to quit if he were indeed fired, his employer backed down. But, that didn't mean his employer didn't try more subtle manipulation—all to no avail. My son later told me, "I told them I had survived having to justify my decisions to my mom while I was growing up. I said to them, 'You are no way as tough as my mom!'"

(For the weapons of our warfare are not carnal, but mighty through God to the pulling down of strong holds;) Casting down imaginations, and every high thing that exalteth itself against the knowledge of God, and bringing into captivity every thought to the obedience of Christ. (2 Cor. 10:4–5)

6

HONEST CONVERSATION

During a doctor visit when my son was quite young and about to get a shot, I remember reeling when the nurse told him that he should not worry, that it wouldn't hurt. Her tone was consoling, friendly, and compassionate, but just the same, she wasn't telling the truth. I let him know that it *was* going to hurt, but that I would be there with him. I made a commitment to myself that I would be frank with my children and never engage in misleading them. This led to times when I had to admit my ignorance on certain subjects. Like the time my four-year-old asked me if his bunk beds would be in heaven. He loved sleeping in them, and somehow it was an important thing for him to resolve. I was not as theologically schooled as I am today, but answered, "I don't think so, but I'm sure that when you get there, you'll find that you don't care as much about them as you do now."

It is important for children to develop a sense that they can trust their parents to tell them things as they really are, rather than sugarcoat or mislead them. It is especially important for homeschooling parents as they will have the major share of input into their children's lives and need to establish a foundation of honesty. I am not suggesting that a very young child be burdened with the details of a violent death in the family, but by the same token, whatever is explained needs to be the truth, even if it is a truncated version. Integrity should be the hallmark of the parent/child relationship.

In the academic realm, homeschooling parents need to establish definitive standards in grading and evaluating their children's work, thereby practicing academic honesty. I cannot tell you the times I was tempted to do otherwise when one of my daughters continued to struggle with simple arithmetic. She was truly trying hard, but was literally not making the grade. The temptation was intense to tell her that she had obtained a good mark. Instead, I explained that both of us (teacher and student) needed to go over the material again. Sometimes it took weeks for her to get the 100 percent she wanted so much. Had I given her an "A" just because she tried hard, the actual "A" eventually earned would have had little significance.

The greatest area in which parents need to be more honest with their children has to do with character issues and being frank about their own past sins and shortcomings. Since all of us have a "story" that led to our coming to faith and repentance, it is important that from the time our children are very young, they hear these stories within the context of God's law-word. These can serve as real-life lessons that take on added value because they are part of the family history.

For example, there is a story my children have heard over and over again about how I, as a child, would sit stubbornly at the table and refuse to eat meals I didn't like. Cajoling, persuasion, removal from the table, and making it so one meal (no matter how cold or wilted) was carried over to the next, were frequent occurrences at my house. My stubborn defiance would reach such peaks that my mother, in her frustration, would on occasion take the split pea soup or whatever I was defiantly refusing to eat and bring me into the bathroom and dump it on my head over the bathtub. (My healthy hair over the years may be due to this unusual composting!) Apparently it was quite a spectacle, one that my older brother and sister relished. I can recall one day when they were particularly gleeful over my impending doom and recited all-too-audibly for my mother to hear, "Hail Mary, full of grace, I hope she gets it in her face." Much to their surprise, they were the proud recipients of my uneaten meal!

My children laugh hysterically at this account, picturing me with food on my head. Each of them was originally introduced to this story as a result of manifesting stubborn defiance. By using my own sinfulness as a real-life example, I was able to impart an important lesson at an appropriate time. I additionally explained that my mother's solution was not a Biblical one and that her frustration grew out of not exercising God-ordained remedies. You see, I wasn't afraid to let them know that I had been a stubborn child. I maintained the fact that I, too, was a sinner and could well identify with their own rebellion, but as a parent it was my job to apply God's Word to our lives. Additionally, this story serves as a good lesson in not being happy when a brother or sister is under discipline. The picture of my siblings with *my* food on *their* heads brought the point home quite well.

By the time children have been around for a decade or so, they often conclude that their parents are "out of touch" with their feelings or concerns. This is where a steady diet of a parent's stories (times when the right choices were made and times when they weren't) accomplishes two things. First, the child realizes that mom and dad were young once themselves. And, second, the parent is not hindered by the concern that he or she is being hypocritical ("I did stuff like that when I was a kid. Who am I to talk?"), but rather knows it is a faithful approach to uphold "Thus saith the Lord."

Parents should be able to look into their children's eyes and honestly, without hesitation, proclaim they have never intentionally lied to them nor led them to believe something that wasn't true. All the more reason for parents to be faithfully reading, learning, and applying the Word of God to their lives so that when times of defiance come from their offspring, they are not stumped as to applicable teaching or hampered by past misdeeds of their own.

I don't imagine parenting has ever been an easy calling. There is a measure of humor in realizing that all of us began life as children ourselves. So, there is little room for sanctimonious attitudes on our part when it comes to admonishment or correction. So, look into your own past and evaluate the thoughts, words, and deeds from your past and get ready to begin a "Once upon a time …"

> *Let your light so shine before men* [and especially your homeschooled children], *that they may see your good works* [faith and repentance], *and glorify your Father which is in heaven.* (Matt. 5:16)

7

HELPING YOUR
CHILDREN FAIL

Know ye not that they which run in a race run all, but one receiveth the prize? So run, that ye may obtain. And every man that striveth for the mastery is temperate in all things. Now they do it to obtain a corruptible crown; but we an incorruptible. (1 Cor. 9:24–25)

We live in an age of superstars. Whether it is sports, academics, entertainment, or politics, at any given moment in time there is usually a "big name" that defines success in a particular area of life or an endeavor. In such an atmosphere, where competition maintains an ever-present role, there are, almost by definition, more *losers* than *winners*. Since parents are not able to single-handedly alter the makeup of the society that their children have been born into, assisting their children in their inevitable "defeats" is an important role of parenting.

Competition, and the resultant designation of first, second, or third place, often gets a "bad rap" in Christian circles. In some homeschooling circles, competition is practically defined alongside immodesty or abuse. One hears comments such as, "Why do there have to be winners and losers? Can't we just play and not keep score?" Or another common refrain (usually uttered when a child has not performed well in some activity), "Well, we just want him to have fun." Or, "My child is not a good test taker; she does not do well under pressure."

Whether it is a game of checkers, chess, or monopoly, a golf tournament, or a speech and debate competition, there *will* be winners and losers. That's how the games are set up and what makes them endeavors that have value above and beyond their outcomes. For in playing competitive games, we all learn how to win and how to lose within the confines of rules and allotted times. With the proper perspective, these excursions into competition help us to see how we act and react under pressure: do we indulge in negative thoughts and self-deprecating remarks when things go poorly? Do we tend to blame others for our costly mistakes? Are we nasty when it looks as though we won't prevail?

I've yet to meet anyone who *likes* to lose at anything, and yet if we as Christian parents neglect to prepare our children for the inevitable times of "failure" by sheltering them from contests that not only test their ability to perform, but also their underlying character qualities, we leave them unprepared for the contests they will face as adults and in their God-given callings. So, along with the subjects you have as part of your core curriculum, I strongly advocate some competitive activities such as music, drama, and sports in which your children's performance will be objectively judged. Knowledgeable parents will learn to expect that initial attempts won't result in a perfect score or outcome. Relish these times as teaching moments for you and your child to determine his strengths and shortcomings in the activity. Was anger a part of the poor performance? How about lack of adequate preparation? Was another competitor just more skilled and more experienced? Did failure to abide by the rules result in the defeat? Answering those questions takes the "mystery" out of winning and losing and relegates it to its proper role—how one fared in a particular contest in relation to the standards of that activity.

I spend a good portion of my summer months taking my daughter to golf tournaments. When we arrive at the golf course, before we exit the car I remind her that whether she scores a 68 (that would be a great score in golf) or a 108 (that would be a really bad score for her at this point), I promise to take her home, feed her dinner, and allow her to sleep in her room. (As ridiculous as this may sound, not all parents are this easygoing!) I also remind her that her salvation is not at stake, although her Christian witness is. Then, when the competition is over, we talk at length about how she performed and what areas she can improve upon. Most importantly, we evaluate whether she let her light shine before those in attendance so that they would see her good works (demeanor and attitude toward fellow competitors, their parents, and the officials) and glorify her Father in heaven. Over time, her performance on the course has improved, as has her ability to deal with interim failure, admit her mistakes, and receive constructive criticism.

Most successful people I've spoken to or read about admit to learning much more about themselves through their failures than their successes. In a very real sense, one can't really be prepared to succeed if one is afraid to fail. For God's people to succeed in the tasks He has laid before us, we need to practice engaging in challenging contests, living with the outcomes, and learning from the particulars. Only then will making disciples of all nations be something we can pursue with excitement and the confidence that our and our children's *less-than-perfect* results are not really failures, but *successes-in-training*!

8

CHARACTER MATTERS

If I profess with the loudest voice and clearest exposition every portion of the truth of God except precisely that little point which the world and the devil are at that moment attacking, I am not confessing Christ, however boldly I may be professing Christ. Where the battle rages, there the loyalty of the soldier is proved, and to be steady on all the battlefield besides is mere flight and disgrace if he flinches at that point.

—*MARTIN LUTHER*

I can recall reading this quote for the first time. Its message along with the context in which it was being quoted had the quality of a double-edged sword that penetrated deep into portions of my soul. It eloquently described a battle I often found myself in as a homeschooling mom. It brought with it an accompanying conviction that the whole endeavor of homeschooling indeed involves warfare of a spiritual nature.

I began my homeschool journey for good, but immature, reasons. As I gained more knowledge of my faith and experience as a teacher, my reasons matured and the practice got easier. I thus felt it was going to be smooth sailing from that point on, since all the basics were covered and a good foundation had been laid. After all, I had excellent curriculum, a good schedule, and support from family and fellow believers. What I didn't anticipate were the battles for the Kingdom of God that would be fought at my kitchen table daily. Battles that would be over the "ground" of by what standard we would live. Could we keep *most* of God's law-word and still be okay with Him? Would we accept His holy standards and decrees of the way things are and the way things ought to be?

Even after almost twenty-five years of homeschooling (am I tenured yet?), the enemy still shows up to challenge me. How? Well, just today during math class I was pointing out an error to my student. She doesn't like getting her problems wrong (who does?) and snapped at me as I was showing her the mistake. The student of my dreams says, "Thanks, Mom. I appreciate it when you teach me." The student of my reality sneered and said, "Why do you have to use that tone of voice? Give me my paper back; I'll figure it out myself!"

You see, I then and there had a choice to make. Do I ignore the insolence and attitude that clearly is a mark of disrespect and lack of honor (violation of the Fifth Commandment) OR do I decide that getting through this math lesson is more important because I have other things to do such as laundry, writing, balancing the checkbook? Well, the *flesh* part of me says, *Let's just get through the lesson so that we can be done.* The *Holy Spirit* within me convicts, *No, now is the time to address her heart with Scripture and its principles because those are the things that will inform her mind, her speech, and her actions.* In other words, this is where the battle was raging *today*!

Let me assure you that the second way takes much more time and energy to perform—often making it so that my to-do list has many unchecked items at the end of the day. You see, after the reproof comes the teaching, then the reconciliation, and finally the resumption of whatever it was that sparked the incident in the first place. Let me also assure you that each and every time I'm faced with this sort of situation, everything within me wants to take the shortcut approach. However, I've learned that character lessons that are overlooked come back to haunt both me and my child/student and will eventually have to be learned anyhow. It's my position of *mother/teacher* that overrules my preference as a *woman with more things to do already than I have time for* that dictates my approach.

In the long run, I've received thanks and commendations from my older children/students for having held my ground under such circumstances. They have pointed out that when they entered the workplace, they were in a much better position to submit to authority and have God's Word come to mind as they were faced with trying situations. In fact, they confide in me (years later, of course) that in the midst of their corrections as students, they were grateful they had a mom/teacher who cared enough to establish the fact that in our home character mattered.

9

CONSOLIDATION OF EFFORT

Okay, so now you have convinced yourself that maybe, just maybe, this homeschooling undertaking that you've begun has a real chance of working out. You've got your mission statement in place, and you've purchased some materials to work with. A tentative schedule has been posted, and you've even called yourself a teacher to someone who asked you today at the gym what you do for a living. So, exactly how are you going to cover all the subjects with your multiple students and get it all done in the six hours your kids would normally be in school?

The answer: you don't! Homeschooling is not "outside school" (as my son used to call it) and does not need to take its cue from what goes on in traditional classrooms. Students don't have to sit in their seats and raise their hands to ask questions. Bathroom breaks can happen as needed. If it's rainy and cold outside, pajamas, slippers, and robes are suitable uniforms. And (this is the part my kids always grumbled about) if one of your students is slightly "under the weather," school can still take place—possibly in front of the TV watching science or history videos or reading in bed.

What about children in the family who are not in the same grade? How does a homeschooling parent find the hours in the day to teach different grade levels for math, science, history, language, and more? The answer: you don't! Smart veteran home educators tackle subjects like history and science by paying less attention to grade level and more attention to group opportunities to read aloud or listen to audio or VHS tapes. Surely your fourteen-year-old will grasp more than your eight-year-old. However, the ensuing discussion and the learning that come from hearing others' perspectives makes the subject one that benefits students of all ages. I can remember listening to history tapes in the car as we traveled back and forth to our extracurricular activities when my two older children were fifteen and eight years old. Just in case I had any concern that they weren't understanding the subject matter, the discussion at the dinner table disabused me of that. My husband used to comment that we would "fight the war between the states" at the dinner table, as each would give his or her case for who was right and who was wrong.

While we are on the subject of the dinner table, in my home/school—aside from when we all sit down for dinner as a family (maybe two to three times per week)—reading is allowed and even encouraged at the table. Not only does much good literature get devoured along with their breakfast and lunch, but I use that time to catch up on reading that allows me to be a better and well-informed teacher.

Also, I found early on that I could combine subjects that day schools often separate. For example, once my daughter learned her letters and needed to practice her cursive, instead of just practicing from a workbook, she had to copy the questions and answers from the Westminster Shorter Catechism. Not only was she getting handwriting practice, but she would say the questions and answers aloud as she wrote them and was memorizing them in the process. When my husband was dismayed that our son's handwriting was proving to be as bad as his own, he had him transcribe the book of Genesis, having him present his notebook daily to ensure that it was readable.

Then there is the flexibility to turn everyday or mundane tasks into learning experiences. For example, when our dog was scheduled to have her spaying surgery, I asked the veterinarian if we could come in and observe. Having prepared my two girls (seven years apart in age) for what we were going to witness, they each got a firsthand view (albeit with different levels of understanding) of what is involved in surgery.

The key to a successful homeschooling experience is NOT to fall in love with your schedule and plan to the point that you can't change it or alter it to suit you and your student(s) better. Should you feel you need some outside verification that your children are learning, there are standardized tests that can be purchased or administered by outside groups. The most important areas of testing will be listening comprehension and reading comprehension since these are the ways people learn things. Should you find that the scores aren't what you'd hoped for, take that as an indication that you need to find new ways to cultivate understanding, making sure that your student can explain what he is learning.

God has made us with the desire to know and understand the world around us. You saw that when your children first learned to speak and asked questions over and over again in order to know what something meant or how to do a certain task. Cultivated properly, this is not something that people grow out of. Rather, it is something that is often squelched and buried by making learning drudgery rather than an adventure. You will discover that you will know how much your students are learning, not by the answers they give, but by the questions they ask.

10

LEARNING IS A PRIVILEGE, NOT A RIGHT

Most parents can relate to the following dialogue (or some variation), often taking place while shopping:

> Child: Mom, can I have those sunglasses?
> Parent: Where are the sunglasses I bought you last year?
> Child: I don't know. But I need some. Will you buy them for me?
> Parent: No, but you have money. Buy them for yourself.
> Child: Forget it.
> [*No purchase made.*]

I've had that conversation more times than I can adequately count. When *I* was buying, my children were more than willing to receive. When it came time for *them* to shell out some of their cash (whether earned or received as a present), they were much less likely to make a hasty purchase. What's my point? Simply put: something that one earns is deemed far more valuable than something just given.

In a homeschool setting, it is very easy for the students to slip into the mode that they are doing their parents a favor by studying or learning a subject. After all, the entire day and the structure of the household are geared toward making learning a part and fabric of home life. Each of my children over the years has slipped into an attitude of entitlement—as though he or she were owed the educa-

39

tional opportunity that was being provided. Moreover, the children would manifest this gross misconception at times by showing disrespect for me as a teacher and failing to abide by my rules and deadlines when it came to academic areas. The more I tried to *explain* and *persuade* how and why their behavior was unrighteous, the less impact it had on them.

One day, I came up with a plan that proved to be effective in handling my stubborn, defiant student who was refusing to learn— I simply suspended him from school! At first, he looked at me with a joyful disbelief as if to say, "*My penalty is that I don't have to do any school today?*" I turned that grin around quickly when I then told him to go to the bathrooms and clean the toilets and to return to me when he was done. From there he progressed to cleaning out closets, washing windows and floors, cleaning the oven and refrigerator, and other not-so-pleasant tasks. I reminded him that if he refused to learn, certain options would be closed to him and I was preparing him for what he might have to do to make a living as an adult.

At first, he would handle a job and then say, "Okay, what's next?" But after a couple of days he was tired of having little time to read or take part in the aspects of schoolwork he did enjoy. He would ask if he could "go back to schoolwork." My response was to give him another job. Finally, he went to his dad and asked if he could go back to school, fervently requesting that he intercede with me on his behalf. When my husband approached me, we both agreed that the lesson had been learned; however, I told my husband with an impish grin, "I really do want that garage cleaned up. Can't I make this go one more day?" So, after that task was completed (and quite well, I might add), my student was reinstated.

It was only after having the *usual* become the *unusual* that he valued his school time. In other words, now it was *his* time that was being spent, and he placed a higher value on spending his own time than he had placed on wasting mine. Moreover, he eventually realized (over time) that the benefits he was receiving of one-on-one academic training would make it so that when it came time to choose his occupation, stronger academics would provide him with greater options than manual labor.

Over the years, my other two children earned their chance at being suspended. Some suspensions lasted longer than others, but weren't complete until I had a student who was taking as much responsibility for learning as I was taking for teaching. Moreover, since they had witnessed the previous sibling's ordeals, many of the lessons had already been learned vicariously.

People (including children) value what costs them something. Learning is a privilege, not a right. Combine these two maxims with the reality that our salvation is very much a privilege rather than a right and you begin to see how our faith must permeate all aspects of our lives and thought. If one doesn't see or feel the need to be saved, the message of the gospel is foolishness to him. If one doesn't see the need to learn and be able to utilize instruction for the glory of God, then academics becomes a punishment rather than a blessing. Education must be a deliberate enterprise, rather than one in which children are "tricked" or "coddled" into participating in the activities designed to make them useful for God's Kingdom.

Homeschooling allows parents to provide a royal education for their children, similar to how kings and queens in the past prepared their offspring to rule in their stead. As children of the King of kings, we should value the opportunity and circumstance we've been given to do the same, being careful not to allow this high calling to be demeaned in any way—especially by our children.

II

MAKING THE GRADE

One of the first things homeschooling parents need to acquire, before buying curriculum or creating a pleasant teaching area in the home, is a homeschooling mindset. Many start out with the idea that they need to outdo the public or private school down the street in matters of learning environment, computers, furniture, and other "outside-school" paraphernalia. While eventually these things will all need to fall into place, without a grounded perspective that establishes the homeschool as a distinct entity, the parents may become sidetracked and their intended results can easily become matters of secondary or tertiary importance.

What exactly is a homeschool mindset? Well, it includes the answers to the following questions:

- Why am I homeschooling in the first place?
- How will I measure success or failure?
- What is my working definition of "education"?
- Who is the authority I will answer to?

To be sure, there are many reasons why parents might decide to take the homeschooling route. However, I recommend that they clearly establish at the outset (possibly putting it in writing) why and how they came to their decision. Whether the reasons were spiritual, physical, emotional, financial, or some combination thereof—or whether parents choose to homeschool as a response to a problem or to follow through with a particular vision—creating a *de facto* "mission statement" will keep them *on purpose* and *on track* toward their goal.

Measuring success or failure is a tricky issue because our culture tells us that we need to be specially trained for years and years in order to teach another human being how to read, compute, and study. Yet, many "products" of this conventional "wisdom" can't really read, comprehend, or utilize the subject matter they are fed for twelve long years of schooling. So, it is imperative that parents have a good working definition of education. *Webster's* 1828 dictionary definition is quite thorough and comprehensive:

> *The bringing up, as of a child, instruction; formation of manners. Education comprehends all that series of instruction and discipline which is intended to enlighten the understanding, correct the temper, and form the manners and habits of youth, and fit them for usefulness in their future stations. To give children a good education in manners, arts and science, is important; to give them a religious education is indispensable; and an immense responsibility rests on parents and guardians who neglect these duties.*

Therefore, an honest evaluation of progress should take into consideration much more than tests results, essay answers, and the like.

Then there is the question of accountability. In other words, where does the "buck" actually stop? Quite apart from the legal requirements of particular states and counties (which are rendering to Caesar what he demands), there is a much *higher authority* that parents will have to answer to in time and eternity. Their standards must remain high and be in accordance with the law-word of God. Choices of subjects studied, athletic activities pursued, or extracurricular activities ventured into, must all be evaluated in terms of preparing children for their God-given callings. Parents must remember that it is the Lord God who gave them their children and whose requirement it is to steward their lives in accordance with His will.

Sometimes homeschooling rookies are way too hard on themselves, certain that their students are falling behind and thereby becoming increasingly separated from the "real world." Some longer in the ranks get weary because they lose sight of the original and/or expanded vision of what they are trying to achieve through their homeschool. I like to challenge and encourage homeschooling parents with this perspective: *We are living and dealing in the real world. It's those who ignore, forsake, or repudiate the God of the Bible and His requirements for learning and living that are dwelling in a fantasy world.* When all is said and done, the "ultimate report card" for parents will be hearing the words of our Savior, "Well done, good and faithful servant."

12

FIT TO TEACH?

I am repeatedly asked the following questions when people discover that I homeschool my children. "Can you do that? Don't you have to have special credentials?" In essence, they are asking if I am qualified for what it is I say I do. Although my *career* as a home teacher has been one of progressive achievements and successes, there are times when I've taken to heart those same questions and wondered, *Am I fit to teach?*

Home teaching involves three basic requirements: calling, capability, and perseverance.

Without a call to this endeavor, the enterprise of home teaching is doomed to mediocrity, calamity, and most certain failure. Frankly, the amount of commitment needed to sustain a home school requires the bolstering of the assurance that one is following the Lord's will. It is not sufficient that all the "experts" tell you that you *should* be called. More importantly, one needs to *hear* the call in Scripture and through prayer.

No one called to this endeavor is unable to become qualified for the task. Some (like me) have had the benefit of a good, solid educational foundation and don't find the academics imposing. There are those, however, who recognize their deficient education and need to make themselves proficient for the role of teacher. Those who begin early in their children's lives have the preparation time necessary to define and refine the subjects they wish to have their children learn. For those whose children are school age or attending school already, the task is greater but not impossible. Like all important pursuits, proper time allocation and prioritizing, along with good curriculum selection and mentoring can reduce the seemingly insurmountable to the merely challenging.

No one called and made capable to this endeavor can succeed without stamina and staying power. But, how does one find the necessary perseverance when multiple children require faces washed, disputes settled, rides to various activities, and questions answered; when the house screams to be cleaned, groceries beg to be purchased, and laundry beckons to be reduced; when a husband (thank God we are only to have ONE) needs his helpmeet to share and assist him in his calling? The answer for me lies in staying spiritually, maritally, mentally, and physically FIT.

Spiritual fitness is accomplished by daily prayer and study in the Word of God along with solid pastoral teaching. Marital fitness is addressed by maintaining the husband/wife relationship as the most important one in the family. This involves having the time to settle differences and ensure that both are praying in unison so that their prayers are not hindered. It has been correctly stated that children's security is provided by the assurance of the love that their father and mother share. Regular times alone must be given priority and the children should make every effort to see to it that obstacles to such time are removed in order to give their parents these opportunities.

Staying mentally fit is more of a challenge. With all the requirements on the homeschool teacher, when can one find the time? The answer is to *make the time*. Without the teacher remaining a student, instruction becomes stagnant and lifeless. Keeping up with current events through good newsletters and periodicals, along with study to prepare for future subjects needing to be taught, is excellent mental stimulation. That way, there is more to talk about than workbooks, multiplication, laundry, and dishes when one is interacting with friends and family. Also, I have found it particularly rewarding to learn new things, as this helps me work to make my presentations more interesting for my students/children.

Physical fitness has rewards that have been widely publicized. However, for the homeschool teacher there are additional benefits to physical fitness. The most important factor is finding an activity that is enjoyable, good in a cardiovascular sense, and doable—one that leaves you ready to return to the demanding job of parent/teacher. I have found that being somewhere other than at home to do this *kills two birds with one stone*. I get away from my "charges" and they get time away from me. We *all* need this time. The hour or two I am away, provides me with sufficient diversion so that I am better able to face the many responsibilities I have. This also gives me valuable insights into teaching itself. Back in 1985 after my second child was born, learning karate to get back in shape forced me to remember what it was like to struggle to master something new. The same thing happened when I took up lap swimming after my third child came along. Now with tennis, I am again challenged to be patient as I become proficient at something that doesn't come naturally to me. This has helped me identity with my children as they've faced problems grasping fractions, geometry, or a foreign language. By assuming the role of student, I find that I am more sensitive as a teacher.

I can almost hear the objections now: *That may all work out well for her, but my situation is totally different.* No doubt it is; however, in assessing your calling and taking each step in its turn, success is likely. And, as a good friend likes to remind me, *success breeds hope.* When all is said and done, the homeschooling teacher may be in the best shape and the most FIT to be a godly parent as well.

13

WHOSE DISCIPLES ARE THEY?

And Jesus came and spake unto them, saying, All power is given unto me in heaven and in earth. Go ye therefore, and teach all nations, baptizing them in the name of the Father, and of the Son, and of the Holy Ghost: Teaching them to observe all things whatsoever I have commanded you: and, lo, I am with you alway, even unto the end of the world. Amen. (Matt. 28:18–20)

But ye shall receive power, after that the Holy Ghost is come upon you: and ye shall be witnesses unto me both in Jerusalem, and in all Judaea, and in Samaria, and unto the uttermost part of the earth. (Acts 1:8)

Homeschooling is much more than a method of educating children; it is a way of life. It sometimes takes a while for homeschooling families to fully appreciate what that means. But eventually they understand that education is something that is an *ongoing* part of life, not something reserved for the months of September through June or to be compartmentalized into subjects such as mathematics, science, history, or literature and jammed into an 8:00–2:30 time frame. The comprehensive nature of the endeavor involves a world and life view that elevates all activities to either "learning activities" or activities where what one has learned is being applied. More than anything else, homeschooling is an excellent method whereby parents can obey the Great Commission as it applies to their children. The main task of producing disciplined individuals who know and apply the law-word of Jesus Christ in their daily lives is more than anything else an activity of discipleship.

I was able to see firsthand evidence of this recently in my younger daughter as she and I traveled back to New York to attend a family funeral. Many had never met her before, and those who had were surprised to see how much three years of growth had accomplished. Sure, there were the expected, "My how tall you are!" and "How pretty you've become!" But repeatedly I heard from friends and family alike how impressed and "blown away" they were with her maturity, poise, and demeanor at thirteen years old. The interesting part is that she was just acting like herself. This wasn't her best behavior—this was her customary behavior.

What were the elements that brought rave attention and kudos to me as her mother?

- The practice of looking adults in the eyes when she spoke with them
- The habit of addressing people by name and being interested in their life and concerns
- The willingness to chip in and help even before asked to do so
- The practice of checking with me prior to accepting something offered to her to make sure she had my approval
- Her willingness to talk about things she was doing in her life (repeatedly as she met new people) in an interested and agreeable fashion, regardless of whom she was talking to
- Being put on the spot by relatives, and yet respectfully conducting herself in a way that honored them

True, these are things that well describe my daughter, but I've also just described a multitude of homeschooled students I've known over the years I've been involved in home education. In other words, my daughter is far from being the exception; she is more like the rule.

It is a sad commentary on our times when manners and respect for elders (behaviors that used to be taken for granted) are now viewed as extraordinary. However, one need not look too far to discover why this would be. Subjecting children to the teaching that there are no moral absolutes, that they evolved from apes, and that Jesus Christ has no place in their world of learning and life are good places to assign the blame. Yet, it is a sadder commentary that many well-meaning Christians continue to allow their children to be fed a steady diet of anti-Christian materials and instruction in public schools, without *significant* measures employed to counteract the deleterious effects. From my point of view, if you are going to have your children in secular schools, you better spend *more* time instructing them as to the Biblical point of view rather than *less*. From that standpoint, homeschooling becomes the choice that takes less time and effort. It is far easier to impart the truth from the outset of learning a subject when no falsehoods have to be tackled and removed, rather than after many years into the indoctrination.

As parents, we need to obey the Great Commission (making disciples) first and foremost with our own children. Their responses to the world in which they live, the material that they are studying, and the issues that they face all need to be formulated from a Biblical mindset. That task is something that takes years and years of instruction, application, testing, and refinement, and is best done by Christian parents discipling their own children. You see, first your children should be your disciples, and as they grow and mature, they'll come to realize that they, along with you, their parents, are disciples of Jesus Christ.

Whose disciples are your children?

14

THE ROD OF DISCIPLINE

He that spareth his rod hateth his son: but he that loveth him chasteneth him betimes. (Proverbs 13:24)

Foolishness is bound in the heart of a child; but the rod of correction shall drive it far from him. (Proverbs 22:15)

I hope I'm not disappointing you, but this is not going to be an essay on spanking. Having been both on the giving and receiving end of this practice, I am personally convinced of its merits, both as a child and as a parent. My focus on the rod, while it takes into consideration the verses referenced above, is more in line with the way it is used in Psalm 23:4, which reads, "Yea, though I walk through the valley of the shadow of death, I will fear no evil: for thou art with me; thy rod and thy staff they comfort me." There is an obvious allusion here to a shepherd tending his flock, and the rod and staff are among the tools of his trade, if you will, that allow him to do the job he has been entrusted to do. Homeschooling parents also have similar tools at their disposal to steward the lives of the child(ren) the Lord has blessed them with—a rod and staff to *comfort* them.

It is customary in our modern culture to encourage self-esteem in children. Note that this is quite different than teaching them to respect other people in their speech and actions; thereby will they know that as they honor God, they will develop a proper image of themselves. Self-esteem, as it is currently defined, is all about *liking oneself*. However, that begs the question as to whether or not any individual has good reason to esteem himself. In fact, we know that there is that nasty blot of sin that, without the Redeemer's blood, makes it so there is nothing much to esteem, let alone like, in our nature. So, a parent's job is more to develop a proper sense of duty and responsibility in a child, and have *those* things bring about a child's proper view of himself.

Homeschooling situations provide regular hands-on, one-on-one situations whereby the homeschooling mother must make good use of the "rod" and the "staff" to prod and corral her student(s) to persevere through a subject or activity that is proving difficult. This prodding can take a variety of forms, and is often accompanied by the child/student glaring at and making irritated/irritating faces at the mother/teacher! Most likely, the shepherd in managing his sheep does not resort to screaming and yelling as his main tools. The Scriptures point out that sheep know their shepherd's voice (not his yells) and respond to his authority, care, and love. Throughout the pages of the gospel narratives, Jesus gives us this shepherd/sheep analogy over and over. As parents, we need to imitate our Savior when it comes to shepherding the sheep He gave us. Thus, as we discipline our children, we need to be careful to differentiate willful disobedience from the sinful nature (and all its manifestations) that came with them at birth.

For example, my daughter is a competitive golfer, and I often accompany her during practice times. Golf can be a frustrating game, even to someone good at it, and there are times that errant shots or unintended consequences have produced angry reactions, which only serve to make the next shots even worse. As a parent, I realize that she is not trying to get angry; rather, the situation is making her angry. However, I also realize that unchecked, this can and will develop into a pattern of angry responses to adverse situations—something I know is unbiblical per Proverbs 22:24, "Make no friendship with an angry man; and with a furious man thou shalt not go."

So, how do I use my rod and staff to comfort her in these situations—her "valley of the shadow of death"? (Note: mathematics also has had the ability to produce similar teary eyed, eruptive responses!) Simply put, I continue to put forth the standard that the activity we're involved in has value over and above itself. I emphasize that this struggle is being given to her by God for the express purpose of refining her—removing the dross and leaving the refined gold. If she wants to quit the activity in the midst of defeat, I refuse to let her. If she tries to wiggle out of the situation by deciding she is stupid or incapable, I hold her "feet to the fire" and make her produce even a somewhat positive result. In other words, I don't let the situation end in failure. Even if that means continuing with the activity an additional hour or two. Keep in mind that I am not trying to produce a golf star or math whiz. I'm attempting to get my daughter to see that she can do all things through Christ who strengthens her. And, that no temptation has or will seize her that is exclusive to her, and that she can be sure Christ will provide the way out for her by means of His grace.

The point here is that the parent/teacher isn't there to build up the child/student's self-esteem. Our job as parents is to mold and shape the youth of today for the tasks that adulthood has in store for them tomorrow. The only real accolade that matters, and will produce the greatest "self-esteem," will come from the mouth of our Lord:

> *Well done, thou good and faithful servant: thou hast been faithful over a few things, I will make thee ruler over many things: enter thou into the joy of thy lord.* (Matthew 25:21)

15

THE HARSH TRUTH

When I began to homeschool, I had no idea of the magnitude or scope of the undertaking with which I was becoming involved. In fact, when I discovered that there were a substantial number of Christians who were pursuing this choice, I was equally amazed. I remember telling my husband, "Guess what? We're accidentally doing the right thing!" Over my almost-quarter-century of experience, I have become a seasoned veteran who often finds herself in the role of homeschool apologist or mentor, depending on the circumstances. I've also been asked by friends and professionals alike to read and crtitique their unpublished manuscripts. So, when the editorial staff of Chalcedon asked me to read a manuscript copy of *The Harsh Truth About Public Schools*, I figured it would be like many other pieces I'd been asked to evaluate. What I didn't expect was how impressed I'd be with a work that was basically stating what I already knew. Now, instead of dreading all the lessons and practices I had to sit through waiting for daughter(s) to be done, I relished the opportunity to make my way through this amazing book. My response to the staff at Chalcedon was, "You MUST publish this book! It says all the things I've been observing and commenting on for years. The church needs this book."

When the book finally made its way into print, Bruce Shortt (the author) had already made a name for himself with his resolution within his denomination to have Christian parents remove their children from state schools. Being the idealist that I am, I thought all that would be necessary for Christian parents and pastors (who had yet to embrace the idea of Christian education) to do was *read the book*. I immediately ordered thirty copies of the book, handing it to pastors, home and Christian school educators to pass along to their pastors, and Christian parents whose children were attending public schools. I even mailed a number to certain radio-show personalities I frequently listened to.

I reserved most of the copies for those who are in leadership positions in the church my family and I currently attend. With each one, I included this note:

> Please take the time to look through and read (in part or in whole) this book.
>
> I had something to do with getting this book published, although very indirectly. Four years ago I was given a manuscript version of this book in order for me to give my opinion as to whether or not it was publication worthy. I was selected because I have been involved with Christian education (specifically homeschooling) since 1982.
>
> After reading it, if you feel that you are interested in hearing how I think our church can play a part in helping its members catch the vision for Christian education for our youth, I would be very eager to meet with you.
>
> Thanks for taking the time to consider this.

I'd love to report that I was contacted immediately or even soon after. Instead, after a good amount of time had transpired, I approached various people asking if they had read it, only to be told, "No, not yet." After that, when certain individuals would see me heading down the hallway, they would seemingly avoid me, being in a hurry to do some important task. I even set up a meeting with the pastor for ministry involvement, hoping to be plugged into the church's referral pool for families seeking more information about homeschooling, or to be able to give a lecture or informal talk about how to get started. Even though this was a polite encounter, nothing substantive has come of it. More depressingly, I was told that the church was working on a policy to deal with issues like this one, comparing my request to candidates seeking public office who wanted to address the congregation, or merchants who wanted to solicit business from the church membership.

Why was I so misunderstood in my request? Or was I very well understood, and that really was the issue? Theological underpinnings, skewed priorities, a less than full-orbed reading and application of Scripture are possible answers to these questions. Moreover, in looking at my church and others like it in their approach to evangelizing children, how much sense does it make to bolster the children for one to two hours at Sunday school, only to turn them over to the God-haters for the rest of the week, who will work to undo and uproot the seeds sown? Would we expect people to be healthy and productive if they swam, bathed, and drank polluted water every day except two to three hours on Sunday? Why are our churches so willing to maintain the status quo?

And, not to lay blame only on the institutional church, there are a number of Christian parents I have given the book to who read it (or portions of it) and told me how it convicted them, but who have decided to keep their kids in public schools—even after enumerating for me the accuracy of Mr. Shortt's description of the social, physical, academic, and spiritual assaults on children found in the local school in their nice suburban neighborhood. Again, why are families so willing to maintain the status quo?

I don't presume to have the definitive answer, but I do have words of encouragement to those who are contemplating or have already embarked on this homeschooling experience. Your audience is and will always be the triune God and the great cloud of witnesses who are cheering you on to run your race. The fruit of your efforts, while not always looking as choice as you would hope, will be pleasing to your Creator as you work to train up your child in the way he should go (in all areas of life and thought and in all academic subjects) to the end that when he is old, he will not depart from your hands-on teaching of the Word of God. You will also take comfort in knowing that you will avoid the harsh truth that

> ... *whoso shall offend one of these little ones which believe in me [and cause him to stumble], it were better for him that a millstone were hanged about his neck, and that he were drowned in the depth of the sea.* (Matt. 18:6)

16

PAINFUL PARENTING

Over the years, my hair has become grayer, and the forces of gravity have helped establish me as an older woman, one who is deemed wise. Thus, I've had the opportunity and privilege of being consulted for advice when homeschooling parents experience difficulty in raising and rearing their children. Having been a good student of the Bible and having studied the principles of nouthetic counseling (counseling from a thoroughly Biblical perspective), I've been able to help parents "put on the glasses of Scripture" in order for them to see situations more clearly and be better able to deal with their difficult times.

In my own life, I have had more than one rude awakening regarding the perspectives and behaviors of my own children. The question remains, *if I was able to give sound counsel to others in adverse circumstances, how come I wasn't prepared to see similar things happening within my own family?* Currently, I am living out the answer to that question; I am searching the Scriptures for parent/child situations that appropriately speak to this issue and am seeking the guidance of the Holy Spirit and other believers in praying for the return of my prodigal.

I am convinced that one of the main issues we face as parents (and especially homeschooling parents) is raising the kids that God *didn't* give us. Simply put: we have an image of what we want our children to become (according to the principles we have taught them) and then assume that they have embraced these same principles—sometimes when there are significant indications to the contrary. Somewhere along the line, new ideas and influences come into their lives and subtle, but real, shifts begin to take place. For example, what one young girl might find offensive in dress when she was nine now becomes *freedom of expression* at sixteen. What a young man might consider rude and inappropriate speech at ten, now designates him as mature and "cool" to his friends. Did our children change? Or did the circumstances in which they live and move widen and more of their own sinful tendencies begin to emerge?

Regardless of how acceptable and routine homeschooling has become, there still exists much opposition by flesh and blood, let alone principalities and powers in high places. Our enemy is all too willing to concede our children to us when they are young, only to entice us with the idea that a college degree (especially from a well-renowned secular school) will ably prepare our kids for their callings under God. However, statistics bear testimony (as does my personal experience) that this stage of life is among the most vulnerable. It is likely that significant damage can be done and is done to a young person's witness and convictions as they are barraged by the onslaught of secular academia. The words of 1 Peter 5:8 ring out loudly, "Be sober, be vigilant; because your adversary the devil, as a roaring lion, walketh about, seeking whom he may devour."

Homeschooling families (which tend to be larger) have to proceed through this stage with many younger eyes watching. The older child's "acting out" has to be carefully dealt with so that precedent is not established in the younger ones' minds. Hence, in the midst of emotional upheavals, the parents' commitment to the Word of God must remain steadfast.

As I write this, I'm relying on the promises of my Lord and Savior that the good work that was begun in my child will see its fruition in the day of Christ Jesus. In the meantime, rather than doubt the jot and tittle of God's Word, I embrace it more fully. For that is the only Rock capable of supporting this grieving parent who has had to hear the accuser of my soul mock my home-schooling efforts and ridicule my faithfulness to the tenets of my faith.

> *[G]reater is he that is in you, than he that is in the world* (1 John 4:4).
>
> *[L]et God be true, but every man a liar* (Romans 3:4).

17

WHAT TO DO
WITH OUR DAUGHTERS?

I cannot tell you how many times I've had homeschooling Christian moms ask me what they should do with their post-high school daughters. Often, I brace myself to discover what sort of awful situation they have gotten themselves into. But, surprisingly, more often than not, their question centers around what to do with a daughter who wants to continue living at home and who is eager for marriage. When I respond that it sounds like they have a pretty good situation, a sigh of relief often is accompanied by, "I'm so glad to hear you say that!"

What is wrong with this picture? Well, for starters, it is as though there were some mysterious "they" out there who were shaking "their" collective heads disapprovingly at these moms. How conditioned we are by the non-Christian culture around us! The very same moms who successfully got their daughters to the point of being educated, useful, helpful, and productive in their family are suddenly back defending themselves just like they did when they decided to homeschool originally.

I can almost hear the screeches now! Barefoot and pregnant—is that the idea? However, before you condemn my perspective, you should hear me out. I am *not* advocating the barring of girls from higher education, getting a job, or doing any number of productive things. Nor am I saying that every girl will eventually marry (whether they hope to or not). Rather, I'm suggesting that in the natural flow of things the future shouldn't be that daunting. What have they been doing up until now? What have been the areas of training and productivity that have been emphasized? In other words, this moment in time should have been anticipated and prepared for so that the next move wouldn't be a leap—just another step.

I am a firm believer in not eliminating options prematurely. For example, back when my daughter was little, piano was a course of study that she was required to take. I couldn't have known when she was seven whether or not being a performer or teacher was in God's plan for her. So, she continued studying the piano until she was proficient at sight reading (enough to play hymns for the family) and until another area of gifting became more apparent and needed more of her time. Similarly, her understanding of science was not pursued because we felt she was going into research, medicine, or engineering. She was required to learn about and understand science in order to have a good working knowledge of the world in which God had placed her.

Among the many jobs that parents have is the responsibility to steward the lives of the children God has placed in their care. Part of that task is to "study" their temperaments, natural inclinations or talents, and heartfelt desires. By not ruling anything out prematurely, this period of training can be a productive foundation for the future. Then, instead of wondering what to do with a daughter, many potential answers and options should be on the horizon already, because the questions have been asked for some time.

How do your particular daughter's preferences factor in to all this? They are as much a part of the recipe as your input. From the time she is old enough to recognize that people have duties and responsibilities (maybe three or four years old), you should be noting what things she particularly has affinity for and steering her in those directions. It is very beneficial to observe this in your children, as it gives you a window into their hearts and minds. Does this mean that if your ten year old informs you that she's not going to study arithmetic, you tell her she doesn't have to? Hardly. It can be, however, an opportunity for you and her to note that it isn't her forte. Maybe this particular struggle is one of the many lessons God has given her to learn perseverance and patience!

If we communicate to our daughters that their chief end is to glorify God and enjoy Him forever from the time they are young, these sorts of issues, while not easy, can be dealt with much smoother because the context of serving God has always been the major factor in the equation.

What to do with our daughters?

Recognize that they need us now, as much as ever, to continue the good work begun in them by Christ Jesus.

18

LIVING LAB

Our family has always been a homeschooling family. We have had the advantage of not having to undo the mindset imparted to children in government schools. When my son finished the homeschooling segment of his education, he took classes at the local college. Often in life one has to accept what is available, rather than one's ideal situation.

My son found himself in politically correct, relativistic, anti-Christian, anti-human, anti-responsibility classes where everything we attempted to impart was challenged and ridiculed. Rather than embrace the "Babylonian perspective," he had the insights and responses I prayed he would have. He returned one morning from his required English class with the comment, "Without the Bible, everything is allowed." He took this class as a summer student so what would normally take a number of months was accomplished in six weeks of eight hours of instruction each week.

His first oral report was to be on the welfare system, which he spent the previous evening preparing. This particular assignment was to be graded by another student in the class. He had sat through others' presentations and most were given a "B" or higher by fellow students. Right before he got up to give his presentation, the teacher informed him that she was changing his topic. He was to give his opinion as to whether or not homosexual couples should be allowed to adopt children.

He composed himself, thought a bit, and began his presentation from the standpoint that since homosexual marriages were not legal, they should not be allowed to adopt. Little did he know that the individual who was to grade him was a homosexual. Immediately my son was attacked for his views and was told by this practicing homosexual that they were offensive to him. As he continued on with his presentation, the rest of the class fell totally silent. He found himself with the opportunity to speak in terms of the Bible's standards. The student gave him an "F," despite the fact that he backed up his positions and was articulate in his presentation. The teacher allowed the grade to stick.

The following day the topic went to "animal rights." The teacher had the class read an article which stated that Christians were among the worst offenders in violating the rights of animals, due to the fact that they practice animal sacrifice. When my son told the class that he was a Christian and knew that animal sacrifice wasn't part of Christian practice, the entire discussion resulted in an open attack on Christianity. The homosexual made the comment that, "The Bible has some good stuff in it but is responsible for the 'gay-bashing' that goes on today."

The next day the teacher handed out a sheet with a proposition for ending world hunger. The article posited that eating the flesh of dead human beings (because it is so plentiful) was the answer. She asked the class to move into groups as to whether or not they "strongly agreed" or "strongly disagreed" with the idea proposed. Half the class joined the "strongly agreed" section. When my son, who had placed himself in the "strongly disagreed" section, spoke up relating the well-documented fact that many diseases are prevalent in societies that practice cannibalism, the teacher told him that he was speaking up too much and to give others a chance. Even when no one else wanted to speak and he offered up a perspective, she "shut him up."

That night, he wrote an essay discussing the ethics involved in using animals in laboratory experimentation. He did some research via the Internet and discovered that vegetarians and others adamantly opposed to hunting animals and their use in laboratory experimentation, classified themselves in favor of abortion and the use of fetal tissue. As was the custom, the next day he gave his paper to another student to do grammatical and style corrections. The girl who was given his paper got to the part about abortion and stood up and loudly cursed at him and told him that she had had an abortion when she was fifteen years old and what did he know about anything. She went to the teacher and told her, in a very loud voice, that she absolutely refused to have anything to do with his paper because he was so offensive to her. The teacher told her she didn't have to deal with him. The next day, the girl apologized to my son and gave him her paper to read. It dealt with her opinion that any man who opposes abortion should have a vasectomy!

I write this soberly and realize that without God's sustaining mercy, none of us could survive in the climate we now face. However, those of us who find ourselves without tremendous options can rejoice in the fact that our God never leaves us or forsakes us or ever lets us go. My son received a first-hand "education" in how presuppositions are inescapable and come through loud and clear in his teachers. The effect of their philosophies and perspectives are evident and speak to their depravity.

To those who have younger children who will eventually face the situations I have just described, my advice to you is to find and support those Christians who are working to reclaim higher education for the Lord Jesus Christ and assist them by your prayers and with your finances in achieving this very necessary goal. In the meantime, pray for us and others like us that God would empower our youthful Christian soldiers.

19

SCHOOL SPIRIT, OR
DEMONS IN HIGH PLACES?

For many years I tasted the rewards of spending time home-schooling my children. However, I also began to see on the horizon the need for something above and beyond the home-schooling I was providing. I was dismayed at the prospects that were ahead of me. So much so, that my son mistakenly understood me to be against higher education in general rather than higher education as it currently exists in our modern culture. It was apparent to me that by the time he reached "college age," there weren't going to be any good choices that would allow him to live at home and enter into manhood with the support and supervision of his parents.

He began taking courses at the local junior college in the summer. In a previous article, "Living Lab," I outlined some of the assaults on his faith that he endured during his first quarter. He continued at this college only to experience a whole new set of unpleasant situations.

SOME CASES IN POINT

Physics class began with the professor asking how many of the 100 students in the class believed that a god created the universe. About twenty or so raised their hands and he systematically pointed to each one of them as he asserted aloud, "Ignorant! Ignorant! Ignorant!" About fifty percent of the classes that followed had more to do with the "ridiculousness of religion over the truth of science" than general physics, and before long it became obvious this was an *anti-religion class* as much as anything else. During a class well into the quarter, he instructed any students who still maintained their belief in a god to make their way to the campus library and look up "religions of the world" to discover how all of them claimed to be true. He didn't specify what they were to do upon completion; however, they were missing a class lecture and the mid-term was two days away. My son dropped the class because he was convinced that a failing grade awaited him. Discussions with the administration proved unfruitful.

His history class (taken the next quarter) continued the assault on Christianity and things Christian. The Crusades were reduced to the National Football League of its day. The beliefs and teachings of Wycliffe, Luther, and Calvin were held responsible for the American Indian "holocaust," and the Puritans' motivations for settling in America were categorized as merely capitalistic. The professor claimed that racism ranked as the major problem in American culture, but began his classes with racist and ethnic jokes (presumably to show their negative impact). One class involved his bringing up ten "white" students and two "black" students, instructing the white students to circle around the black ones. He then asked the following question in front of the 400 or so students in attendance: "How many here think these two black people are the product of bestiality?" Now that he had gotten everyone's attention, he went on to say that early America was very influenced by the myth that blacks were the products of humans and apes and this was an underpinning for slavery. So much for our schools trying to lessen racial tensions!

My son's speech class (the stated purpose of which is to help students learn to express themselves better), seemed to do little more than polarize the students. In one class, when called upon, my son expressed *his* opinion that abortion was wrong. He never said anything beyond that although he could have and was met after class with a punch in the face from another male student who found the opinion that a woman doesn't have the *right to choose* abortion offensive.

I can only pray that the prospects for higher education get brighter for the Christian young people of our country in the future.

20

THE ADVANTAGES OF HOMESCHOOLING

by Anthony Schwartz

Once upon a time there was a group of young people. Some of them were noble children, but the majority of them were not. They went to a place almost every day where learning supposedly took place. Their teachers indoctrinated them in such a way that they were ill-prepared for life and only interested in doing what *they* wanted to do. They were taught how to do evil things, and a desire for those things was fostered. Eventually, these young people came to a point where they had a choice to make. They could either turn around and attempt to make a recovery, or go down a path from which they would never be able to return. The awful part is that many of them had already made the choice with the help of their teachers to go down the path that would lead to death. Some of them did turn around, not because of what the place of learning had taught, but because of others who helped them see the Truth. Unfortunately, many of them did not live happily ever after.

That is a pretty sad story. But, there is another one that may give you hope. It starts the same way.

Once upon a time there was a group of young people. Some of them were noble children, but the majority of them were not. They were in a place every day where learning took place. In this place their parents taught them and tried to give them the best education possible, and prepare them for a productive, godly life. They taught them how to do good things and stirred up a desire for those things. Eventually these young people had a choice to make— either go down a path that led to life or one that led to death. Some of them went down the bad path and never returned. But most of them had an advantage. Most of them had already made the correct choice at an early age and so they pursued the righteous path. These young people grew up to be like the ones that convinced those of the earlier story to turn around. Fortunately, most of those in this story lived happily ever after.

Enough of storytelling. I am one of those people in the second story. I have been homeschooled for nine years.

I am, also, a very competitive person. Just about everything that I do, I try to set up as a competition. Whether it be schoolwork or even mowing the lawn, I try to set it up as a context to push myself through it and to do as well as I can. My teacher, who also happens to be my mom, can attest that sometimes in my algebra, I get *too* competitive. The pencils just don't start flying on their own. If I were in a regular school setting, I think that I would be more concerned with the mark and how I did in comparison to others rather than with actual learning. Since the purpose of learning is to learn, the best possible way that it can take place is to gear it around the student.

Different people have different hopes, aspirations, and needs. I hope to become a lawyer and so the study of history is something that is emphasized. This is one of the greatest, if not the greatest advantage, of homeschooling. The material is geared around the student, the student isn't geared around the material. Plus, the one-on-one ability of homeschooling increases the learning quality immensely. With homeschooling, any difficulty can be addressed on the spot. If someone is more advanced than his or her age might imply, the material can be increased to challenge the person better. On the other hand, if the person is slightly slow, the work can be changed and molded to fit the person's needs.

A common criticism of homeschooling is the lack of social-ization. This is a myth. Let me tell you about some of the things I do and have done. I have been in plays, choirs, baseball, soccer, basketball, and bowling leagues. I have been involved with karate for seven years. I have been taking piano lessons for six years and participate in recitals two to three times yearly. I am the editor and writer for a publication that comes out every other month that other kids write for, too. I am involved in a Friday co-operative study program that involves me with about thirty other homeschool kids, my age and up, and their families. I am a member of a literary club, and for a while I was involved with a chess club. In my mind, that is a lot of socialization when you also consider the dealings that I have had every single day with others that I run in to. This is not unusual for homeschooling families; in fact, many do even more.

And finally, there is the matter of my Christian faith. I come from a Christian family and homeschooling strengthens it. Many people would say that I am not getting the "full" picture. *They* are not getting the full picture. Public schools teach the many different ways of humanism whereas in homeschool, I learn all subjects to understand the underlying issues, with God's Word as a basis.

I feel it is my duty to speak up and to help the United States of America to the best of my ability as a citizen, and as a child of God to help rebuild and strengthen our collapsing society. I feel that the best way for me to train for this is the path my family and I have chosen. Not only is homeschooling advantageous for individuals and families, homeschooling is of great benefit to our country.

{This speech/essay took first place in the FIGS (Friday Independent Group Study) Program (May 1991), which was a cooperative effort of junior high and high school homeschoolers in Santa Clara County, CA, when the author was thirteen years old. Anthony is now married and successful in business, having been homeschooled all the way through high school.}

21

SUPERNANNIES

Ask anyone in my family and they'll tell you that I don't watch a lot of television on my own, and I do so reluctantly when other family members have "the box" on. I have personally ruined many a show for my children (and husband) over the years, as I was quick to point out the unbiblical worldview being presented or an obvious violation of one or more aspects of God's holy law-word. That said, there is an adage I have repeatedly heard that goes something like this: *Everything is good for something, even if it is just to serve as a bad example.*

A while back, I viewed one of the current "reality shows" with my daughter, which has as its premise a "Supernanny" coming in to help a couple deal with their unruly children. All my years of homeschooling must have paid off. I didn't have to say too much, as my daughter did all the talking for me. In the midst of her laughing at the ridiculous situations, I got to hear comments such as, "If I had ever tried to pull something like that, you wouldn't have stood it for a moment!" "That kid needs a spanking something bad!" "That mother doesn't even talk *to* her kids; she talks *at* them!" Moreover, as the Supernanny (English accented, full-bosomed, and oh-so-perfectly acting like Mary Poppins) took the reins of the household, the mom and dad appeared as though deep magic were taking place before their very eyes. They were so in awe of her methods and techniques that when she took her "mandatory leave" so they would have a chance to apply what they had learned, the overwrought couple doubted their ability to continue in her absence. A cameraman stayed behind in order to provide live feed for Supernanny to watch from a remote location. The "drama" unfolded as the parents were on their own trying to manage their daughters, all the while lamenting their inadequacies. Supernanny remained dutifully glued to her television set, appalled at times, encouraged at others, carrying on a one-sided dialogue to her disciples, "Don't let her talk to you like that!" and "Remember what I told you!"

Supernanny's advice was practical at times, although very humanistic all the time. She presupposed that the children inherently wanted to be good and that all mummy and daddy had to do was reprove them (in a stern voice) for not respecting them as parents. She never offered any genuine reason why they were worthy of respect! Then, when things got really out of hand, it was off to the "naughty stool" where the tirade continued for the four-minute minimum, until the child gave a gratuitous "sorry," which was the "get out of jail card" so long as it was said without a tantrum accompanying it. It was clear that without a foundation in transcendental law—a law that goes beyond child and parent—all that was going on here was bad TV.

But think of the "Supernannies" that many Christian parents hand their children over to five days a week, ten months out of the year, many of whom spend more time with the children than the parents do themselves. These are the ones instilling in children how they should act. Whether it is in secular schools or day-care centers, the object is more about controlling behavior than it is about pointing them to their responsibilities to their Creator. Is it any wonder that disrespect and foul mouths often accompany a twelve-year sentence in such institutions? After all, most children have some sense of their duty to obey when they are young, when parents outweigh them and have the power of withholding love, food, and shelter. But, why should kids submit to parents once they've apparently transcended the need for these basic necessities? This follows logically from the secular training that encourages autonomy and "making one's own way in the world." Modern education inherently programs children to "evolve" beyond their parents.

For education to be classified as faithful to Scripture, parents must impart a sense of a transcendent standard that applies to both parent and child, one ordained by the Living God. Catechizing is a powerful and effective means by which the child learns the doctrines of his faith. So, too, is the memorization of Scripture. However, there is much more to the process. *Every* subject must be evaluated through the lens of the law-word of God in order to be properly understood and applied. The standard must not change based on geographical location, cultural norms, or circumstances. The child must comprehend that God requires obedience in spirit and in truth, in all areas of one's life, and all the time. Most importantly, the child needs to learn that the remedy for sin is not the "naughty stool" and a superficial show of remorse, but the sincere application of "If we confess our sins, he is faithful and just to forgive us our sins, and to cleanse us from all unrighteousness" (1 John 1:9).

In all fairness, I'm quite sure that the discipline and instruction in the faithful Christian household wouldn't draw many television sponsors, viewers, or high ratings for that matter. And, most decidedly, all issues and upsets wouldn't be resolved in the one-hour time slot reserved for Supernanny. No, ours is a multi-generational pursuit that includes believing God's plan and promise of victory. Moreover, our calling does not depend on audience appeal or high salaries on earth. Ours is a calling that involves storing up treasures in heaven!

22

I Want To Be A Mommy

Very often when adults try to engage little girls in conversation, the questions that follow go something like this:

1. How old are you?
2. How do you like school?
3. What do you want to be when you grow up?

I recall a specific time when my youngest daughter was eight years old. We were watching her older sister compete in a golf tournament and some adult volunteers, wanting to be friendly, asked this standard litany of questions. She responded a bit shyly but with a smile, "I want to be a mommy." The grown-ups nodded with a bit of a smirk, discounted her answer as being amusingly immature, and responded, "But what do you really want to do? You know, in this day and age you really need to prepare for something more substantial than that. Girls need something to *fall back on*."

This can be a dilemma for a girl who has been raised in a covenant, homeschooling family. From her perspective, Mommy does quite a lot. She teaches; she manages; she is the one who plans meals and establishes acceptable patterns of behavior. She often acts as the family medical assistant, nutritionist, social coordinator, and more. The depth of the answer, "I want to be a mommy," if understood properly by the questioner, encompasses a desire to be someone who is dependably there to instruct, comfort, serve, and love her family. In fact, Proverbs 31 (which my girls memorized very early on in our homeschool curriculum) gives a job description that could easily leave one out of breath. How sad that our culture relegates it to the position of what you do as a female if you can't do anything else!

I, myself, am repeatedly amazed at the capacity of home-school moms. The homeschool choir *Coram Deo Chorus*, of which I am the founder and administrator, repeatedly provides me with wonderful examples:

> • One mother in our group has raised a family of her own (in fact she is a grandmother) and is currently homeschooling four Russian orphans whom she and her husband adopted more than a year ago. While many women in our culture use this time to "find themselves," this mom is once again beginning the process of stewarding young lives (ages six - sixteen) for the honor and glory of Jesus Christ.

> • Another mom is actively homeschooling her three children while finishing up her nursing degree and taking in other students to tutor in math. She is regularly involved in getting her children to their appropriate destinations for extracurricular activities while remaining present at many of them to ensure she knows and understands what they are involved in and with whom.

> • Then there is the homeschooling mom of six who held the position of music director for our choir for two years. This while managing the doctor visits and special therapy for her youngest, who has special needs. On top of having good students, she manages to have champion swimmers in her young entourage along with very capable violinists. All this while being a key member in her church's music ministry and singing with a regional adult choir.

I could go on and on and never stray too far from the women I come in contact with on a regular basis. These women are not busy trying to *fall back* on anything. Rather, they are actively seeking the well-being of their household while their husbands are out providing for the financial needs of their families. True, some are more naturally gifted than others, but that is not my point. In these cases, and more I could enumerate, these women are utilizing all the education, training, and experience of their past as they pursue a calling that far surpasses a mere job.

It is fashionable today to deride the idea of preparing for being a wife and mother. However, the Biblical perspective is far different. When a woman gets her priorities in order—God, her husband, children, extended family, members of the body of Christ, and out into her community—she becomes a powerful force in the advancement of the Kingdom of God.

Mothers, recognize the privilege you have of rearing your daughters in a homeschool setting. Help them see the many facets of your job, and designate them as your assistants as you manage and run your home. From a very young age, give them tasks and responsibilities that are vital to the smooth running of your family life, letting them understand that you are training them for a vital and important role. I am not advocating the abandonment of academic subjects, but rather placing them in context and alongside practical tasks that foster the ability to produce a well-rounded person and manager.

By allowing your daughters to be ready to "take over the household" in your stead (should illness or other responsibilities make it necessary), you will be doing them a world of good by preparing them to be good wives to their future husbands and mothers to their children. You can accomplish this by giving them repeated opportunities to serve their father. (I have made it a standard practice that my girls are responsible to make their father's lunch on a regular basis, make sure his clothes are ironed, and help prepare his dinner when he arrives late from work if we've already eaten.) Both Dad and Mom have to be willing to "live with the mistakes" (of which we've had our fair share) and praise the positive results in order to make this apprenticeship viable. Finally, incorporate volunteer and ministerial opportunities in your daily schedule. Be sure you share your thinking with your daughters as you make household, business, or other important decisions.

Truth be told, if given the opportunity to rearrange my life in any way I'd like, I would still want to be a mommy.

23

IN PRAISE OF
HOMESCHOOLING MOTHERS

It is not customary to praise a group to which one belongs. However, it is possible to step out of a group enough to appreciate and evaluate the talent and achievements of the group.

Recently, our home fellowship hosted a homeschooling seminar. About sixty persons attended and listened intently for about two and a half hours to a curriculum philosophy and absorbed many practical suggestions for implementing it. After we arrived home, my husband commented how impressive (and somewhat intimidating) homeschooling mothers are. I think he was most impressed with the questions and comments that arose from the audience. The knowledge of various orientations to learning, the experience of teaching different ages at the same time, and the obvious desire to refine and improve teaching skills was apparent. It's not that he hadn't had experience with a home teacher (we have been homeschooling since 1983); it's that he assumed I was the exception rather than the rule. I have received his praise over the years, but his assumption was that I could do all this because I had received a superior education growing up.

Back to my praise of homeschooling moms. Many of the women across the country who have responded to God's mandate to educate their children in the fear and admonition of the Lord did not receive superior educations. Many have had to re-educate themselves in order to educate their children properly. They have managed to accomplish this without the praise of the world or even the credentials of the world. In fact, very many continue to persevere and raise the standard of education in our country not because of taskmasters hovering over them but in spite of those who spend much of their efforts to stop them. They are working to produce the leaders of tomorrow.

It is to God's glory and by His supernatural grace that He has allowed us homeschooling moms to go beyond ourselves. Thanks to His call and strength, many of us are moving closer to the standards proclaimed in Proverbs 31 and we thus need to recognize that our merchandise is good! I know it's difficult to view ourselves this way when the hair is getting gray and the figure reveals our age and the number of children we've had. I know that victory isn't always evident and failure not always distant. However, a proper view of our overall effectiveness in performing the tasks that God has called us to can bolster our courage. Courage needed to recognize that the future of our civilization depends very much on what we do now and how we do it. May God grant us the vision to see the fruits of His victory.

> *I will go in the strength of the Lord God: I will make mention of thy righteousness, even of thine only. O God, thou hast taught me from my youth: and hitherto have I declared thy wondrous works, Now also when I am old and grayheaded, O God, forsake me not; until I have shewed thy strength unto this generation, and thy power to every one that is to come.* (Ps. 71:16-18)

24

THE CHANGING FACE OF
HOMESCHOOLING MOMS

Recently I participated as a volunteer at a local homeschool used curriculum sale that takes place every June, sponsored by a local support group. Aside from giving families a way to get curriculum at a tremendous discount, it also raises money for two men in California who work full time monitoring the many threats that arise each year to homeschooling in the California legislature. This year, I was more of a seller than a buyer, as an earlier cleaning project left me with much to put on sale. So, rather than spend an inordinate amount of time perusing the curriculum materials for sale, while I was doing my volunteering, I got a chance to observe the homeschooling moms at work selecting their tools for next September.

The most amazing part about them, was that they were hard to categorize. I saw women whose children were past schooling age shopping for grandchildren or children in their church they help with homework. I saw moms with children in strollers, on baby slings, or waiting patiently in the hallway gathering up books for multi-grades. I saw young pregnant women and more seasoned pregnant women. I saw young nursing moms and older nursing moms. I saw white women, black women, Hispanic women, Chinese women, Indian women—all having in common the desire to

93

get the right materials for their particular children. I saw home-schooled graduates helping their moms set up and run the sale—not acting as though this was beneath them. I saw dads running in and out checking with their wives to ensure the budget wasn't being strained.

When the sale was over and the hall cleaned, I felt very good for the future of homeschooling. Why? Because there wasn't a celebrity in the entire bunch. Just a collection of everyday people wanting to get the best (at the best price) to ensure a good future for their children. It is with such regular folk that the prospects of our culture depend. Despite the fact that I didn't recognize the majority of participants, in a real sense I felt as though I knew them very well. I could relate to their anticipation and desire to do the right thing by their kids—the hope they were getting *the* materials that would best communicate particular subjects—that in the end, their children would be educated.

Before I left for the evening (yes, I ended up buying some curriculum for my sixth grader despite the fact I told myself I wouldn't spend any money), I did have a chance to visit with some other "vets" of the homeschooling trenches. Interestingly, not all shared my optimism for the future. Some lamented that they didn't have kids to teach anymore and really missed it—not really knowing where to put their talents. Another was dismayed because the type of people homeschooling weren't the same as when she started—and now that her children were grown, she couldn't relate to homeschoolers like she used to. However, even these reactions are positive in the sense that homeschooling hasn't become stag-nant—it is changing and growing—adapting to the new situations and circumstances of today. Probably the most encouraging news is that so many homeschool graduates are now in the process of homeschooling their own children, recognizing it as not only a *possible*, but truly, a most *viable* option for their families.

Homeschooling is keeping pace with the changing face of America. And that is a good thing—because it means that the underlying principles are the driving force—that individual fami-lies are motivating themselves rather than being directed by some centralized entity telling them what to do with their children.

I truly feel that the Christian remnant is alive and well—and planning to embrace the future! Can't wait to see who shows up next year!!!

25

A TRIBUTE TO MY MOTHER

Fifty years ago, I was traveling in comfort in my mother's womb preparing for an October birthday. This upcoming half-century birthday is significant for me, because my mom didn't live to see hers. Back in September of 1969, she died in the middle of the night in a hospital not far from our house. I remember my dad coming into the living room where I was asleep on the couch saying, "Your mother is gone." This was the culmination of years of being bed-ridden and unable to speak or care for herself as a result of the numerous strokes she had suffered.

If you know me, you already know a lot about my mother. She was an educated woman (majored in math and minored in art)—loved to read to her children (I can still remember her voice and her "smell" as I pushed for the seat next to hers when it was story time)—helped us with our homework and helped friends who struggled with theirs—wasn't a fabulous cook, but got by—cleaned house reluctantly—and took yearly Christmas pictures of her children, threatening them with eviction or imprisonment if they didn't "Smile!" In fact, I'm sure that had homeschooling been an accepted practice back then, rather than having us attend Catholic school (the priest in my parents' pre-nuptial counseling told them they would go to hell if they didn't send us to Catholic school), my mom would have been active as a homeschooling mom, even heading up homeschool organizations and running conventions. My mom used to write and direct plays for us to perform for my dad on Thursday nights (the night he came home early), and was always active in our projects for school.

Her opinion meant a great deal to me and I can recall hating to be at odds with her, following her around the house at night until she would give me my good-night kiss. Many of the bad decisions I made in my young adulthood were possible because my mother was no longer there to guide, prevent, or punish me. I know, for certain, that some of my "extended mistakes" would never have progressed beyond exploratory stages, because she would not have tolerated my headstrong rebellion. Many of my attitudes and perspectives on being a stay-at-home mom can be directly attributed to this woman who I only knew for fifteen years and eleven months. She was a woman who didn't do things halfway. So many times I've wished I could ask her some questions about myself as a child, offer sincere apologies for wicked and cruel things I did and said to her, and introduce her to her grandchildren.

Mom, on her birthday, had a tradition where she would send her mother flowers. I took up that tradition for a couple of years before she got sick, only beginning to comprehend the possibilities of a maturing relationship between the two of us. By God's will, that seed never had the chance to fully germinate. Now that I've been a mom for almost twenty-five years and a wife three years longer than that, I have a greater admiration for the many things about my mother that I couldn't appreciate or even perceive as a child.

Why, after all these years, have my thoughts been so drawn to my mother? Why does the life of Marie Tesone Letterese seem more important now than it has for the two-thirds of my life that I have been without her? My guess is that it has something to do with the reality that my own daughter, about to start college, is venturing into a new phase of her life—a phase I faced without a mother to talk to, cry with, and share my innermost feelings. God has given me the sense that as I fulfill this very important motherly function in my daughter Rachel's life, I am honoring the memory and efforts of the one who brought me into this world—and one I hope to be reunited with in the next.

26

How R. J. Rushdoony
Changed My Family

The teacher who does not grow in his knowledge of his subject, in methodology and content, is a very limited teacher, and his pupils are "under-privileged" learners.

The teacher as student is, above all else, a student of God's word. To be a student means to advance and grow.

Our growth in teaching requires our growth through and under the teaching of the Holy Spirit. We must become good learners as a step towards becoming good teachers. Our profession is a very great one in Scripture: our Lord was a Teacher, and the Holy Spirit is our continuing Teacher. We cannot treat our calling lightly, nor grieve the Spirit by abusing our calling.

R. J. Rushdoony, *The Philosophy of the Christian Curriculum*

The Bible accurately identifies the fact that without vision, the people perish. For many of us, our original reasons for home-schooling pale in comparison to the strong motivations we now cling to. Too few of us really knew what was at stake. We began with the Spirit's prompting—in many cases living quite above our stated theology. Without a strong theological, intellectual base, though, well-meaning friends and family, an intrusive school board, or political legislators answering to strong and well-funded lobbies would have knocked us down and in many cases out.

The writings of R. J. Rushdoony (specifically his books on public education, Christian education, and the struggle between Christianity and humanism) provided the necessary guidelines to keep us on track. When my son was young, I would threaten him with sending him to "public school" when he repeatedly failed to adhere to my instruction. However, as a result of Rushdoony's influence, I came to understand the extent of the assault on Christianity and God's law in state schools, and I never threatened again. I realized that my threats would be comparable to telling him that if he failed to listen to me I would abandon him along the side of the road to the care of robbers and thieves.

But Rush's works do more than sound a warning. His *Institutes of Biblical Law* and *Systematic Theology* give homeschooling parents the seminary-like education to allow them the grounding to teach every subject from a godly, orthodox perspective. His experience and expertise led me along paths that reaped tremendous rewards for me and my children. Thanks to his influence and perspective that *every area of life and thought is subject to the law of God*, from the time my children were very little, discussions on daily problems or situations were viewed from the perspective of where (not if) God's law addressed it. Many times our dinner table has been the place of important theological discussions that were undergirded by a solid orthodox base.

But these are personal encounters with a writer and his work. The groundwork Rush laid by spearheading the Christian and homeschool movements, and his participation in landmark cases involving the rights of Christians to educate their children as directed by God, helped me even before I had the blessing to know him. For the work he and those who worked with him did, paved the way for me to be able to homeschool without significant incident or opposition. Additionally, there were the many people who had read his work and heard him speak and began to take dominion in the area of homeschooling support groups, magazines, legal assistance, and writing and designing curriculums. In other words, others built on his work; as a result, there are myriads of good resources available to homeschoolers around the country and the world.

But Rush didn't stop there. He continued to write and challenge Christians to *cast their bread upon the waters*. He was not interested in becoming a celebrity-guru who had followers who followed him blindly. Far from it. He lived humbly, took the time to answer questions (even from children), and challenged people to begin a work in their own area and re-take ground for the Kingdom of God. The quality of the people he drew to himself over the years is astounding. Their books fill my bookshelves as do the works of many great men he often referenced and on whose work he expanded.

There are many home educators to whom I've spoken over the years who have known Rushdoony, the work of Chalcedon Foundation, and read his books. They agree with me that he has served as a prophet and mentor in the arena of homeschooling. Often, when our family meets another that has had the benefit of Rush's teachings, there is an instant camaraderie and depth of understanding that is not always present with those who don't have the same grounding.

R. J. Rushdoony, the Christian, the man, the theologian, the advocate, has had an impact that is growing yearly. God has been gracious to us by giving us one who could help us understand our times and be prepared to apply His law-word to every area of life and thought. This good and faithful servant, we believe, will be remembered alongside other greats of our Faith such as Augustine, Calvin, and Knox. How blessed we were to be given a chance to walk alongside him as he did the work God called him to do!

RECOMMENDED RESOURCES

The Philosophy of the Christian Curriculum
by R.J. Rushdoony

The Christian School represents a break with humanistic education, but, too often, in leaving the state school, the Christian educator has carried the state's humanism with him. A curriculum is not neutral: it is ether a course in humanism or training in a God-centered faith and life. The liberal arts curriculum means literally that course which trains students in the arts of freedom. This raises the key question: is freedom in and of man or Christ? The Christian arts of freedom, that is, the Christian liberal arts curriculum, is emphatically not the same as the humanistic one. It is urgently necessary for Christian educators to rethink the meaning and nature of the curriculum.

The Messianic Character of American Education
by R.J. Rushdoony

In this volume the author answers an important question regarding American history: exactly what has public education been trying to accomplish? Before the 1830s and Horace Mann, no schools in the U.S. were state supported or state controlled. They were local, parent-teacher enterprises, supported without taxes, and taking care of all children. They were remarkably high in standard and were Christian. From Mann to the present, the state has used education to socialize the child. The school's basic purpose, according to its own philosophers, is not education in the traditional sense of the 3 R's. Instead, it is to promote "democracy" and "equality," not in their legal or civic sense, but in terms of the engineering of a socialized citizenry. Public education became the means of creating a social order of the educator's design. Such men saw themselves and the school in messianic terms. This book was instrumental in launching the Christian school and homeschool movements.

Intellectual Schizophrenia
by R.J. Rushdoony

When this book was first published in 1961, the Christian homeschool movement was years away and even Christian day schools were hardly considered a viable educational alternative. This book (along with *The Messianic Character of American Education* were a resolute call to arms for Christians to get their children out of the pagan public schools and provide them with a genuine Christian education. Rushdoony was indeed a prophet. He knew that education divorced from God and from all transcendental standards would produce the educational disaster and moral barbarism we have today.

The Victims of Dick and Jane
by Samuel L. Blumenfeld

America's most effective critic of public education shows how America's public schools were remade by educators who used curriculum to create citizens suitable for their own vision of a utopian socialist society. This collection of essays will show you how and why America's public education declined. It demonstrates that this was an educator-engineered decline of reading skills. The author describes the causes for the decline and the way back to competent education methodologies that will result in a self-educated, competent, and freedom-loving populace.

The Harsh Truth About Public Schools
by Bruce Shortt

This book combines a sound Biblical basis, rigorous research, straightforward, easily read language, and eminently sound reasoning. Whether one is a parent or parent-to-be, pastor, church staff member, or educator, this book has much to offer. It is based, first of all, upon a clear understanding of God's educational mandate to parents. Its second foundation is a thoroughly documented description of the inescapably anti-Christian thrust of any governmental school system and the inevitable results: moral relativism (no fixed standards), academic dumbing down, far-left programs, near absence of discipline, and the persistent but pitiable rationalizations offered by government education professionals.

Faith for All of Life

This official publication of the Chalcedon Foundation is published bi-monthly and sent to all who request it. Its emphasis is to proclaim the authority of God's Word over every area of life and thought.

These resources and additional ones are available online @
www.chalcedon.edu

Printed in the United States
216246BV00001B/2/P